Makin' Room in the Inn

An Advent Study

Makin'
Room
in the INN

*Christmas Hospitality Through an
African American Experience*

An Advent Study

HENRY L. MASTERS, SR.

Abingdon Press / Nashville

MAKIN' ROOM IN THE INN
CHRISTMAS HOSPITALITY THROUGH AN AFRICAN AMERICAN EXPERIENCE

This book is printed on acid-free paper.

Library of Congress Cataloging-in-Publication Data

Masters, Henry L.
  Makin' room in the inn : Christmas hospitality through an African American experience / Henry L. Masters, Sr.
    p. cm.
  Includes bibliographical references and index.
  ISBN 978-1-4267-0371-3 (curriculm—printed/text plus-cover, adhesive - perfect binding : alk. paper)
  1. Advent. 2. African American families—Religious life. 3. Hospitality—Religious aspects–Christianity. I. Title. II. Title: Making room in the inn.
  BV40.M385 2010
  242'.33208996073–dc22

                                                                        2010019672

10 11 12 13 14 15 16 17 18 19—10 9 8 7 6 5 4 3 2 1

MANUFACTURED IN THE UNITED STATES OF AMERICA

Contents

Sweet little Jesus boy, they made you be born in a manger.
Sweet little holy child, we didn't know who you were.
Didn't know you'd come to save us to take our sins away.
Our eyes was blind, we could not see. We didn't know who you were.
Long time ago, you were born.
Born in a manger bare, sweet little Jesus boy.
They treat you mean, Lord. Treat me mean, too.
But that's the way it is down here.
We didn't know who you were.

—African American Spiritual

*H*ospitality finds its deepest and most joyful expression during the Christmas season. I remember distinctly one Christmas when all my relatives had come and we were preparing a good old-fashioned "Grandma meal." My grandmother, who had gone outside to respond to some intruder, came walking back in the house accompanied by a man wearing an old, tattered shirt. The man was also not African American; he was white! Everything stopped at the sight of it all. Grandma broke the silence. She said, "This man is hungry and we are all about to eat. Together!" My grandmother's action demonstrated the gift of hospitality. Hospitality was and is a spiritual gift from God. It was expressed in countless ways by members of my family and in the community in which I grew up. We were always making room for someone.

How different it was for Joseph and Mary, who were told that there was no room in the inn (Luke 2:7). Yet, after their baby was born, Joseph was warned in a dream to take his wife and child and "flee to Egypt" (Matthew 2:13). It was to this land and its people that Joseph and Mary escaped with their new child, Jesus. They found refuge in a society where hospitality was not only offered, but exists as the ethical concept of *ubuntu* (sometimes called *ubantu*): community sharing in which we all have being and meaning because of and for others. They arrived in an African village (Egypt is in Africa) that offered to the Holy Family what my grandmother offered to the stranger that day, the gift of hospitality. The ancient wisdom of Egypt encouraged generosity and the understanding that bread must be shared. Given refuge in an environment that believed "it takes a village to raise a child," Mary and Joseph found warmth and safety from the ruthlessness and monarchical envy of Herod. Here, the baby Jesus would spend his formative years; he would be shaped and prepared for life by this African experience of hospitality.

Down through the centuries, the practice of hospitality has become the cornerstone of existence throughout the African Diaspora. It has been cultivated through the exercise of particular disciplines even in the cruelest of times. It has been nurtured by Africa's children in the womb of racism, the indecency of colonialism, the caldron of slavery, the nexus of segregation, and the insidious classroom of discrimination. The memory of and common experience with a "sweet little Jesus boy," who was treated mean, who "we didn't know who he was," is indelibly etched into the psyche of the black soul. And while all believers everywhere practice a magnified hospitality during the Christmas season, black folk, many of whom continue to operate on the margins of the socioeconomic radar, seeking inclusion and room in the inn, tend to be kinder and happier at Christmas than any other time of the year—even when they're broke and out of a job! We can't help but open up our hearts, our doors, our kitchens, and our pockets in unimaginable ways. Buttressed by an indomitable spirit, black people have found a way "when there is no way" to be used of God, time and time again, to make the world better. Contrary to media focus on negative behavior, welcoming the stranger, praying for enemies, doing good to persecutors, encouraging the downhearted, weeping with those who weep, and laughing with those who laugh are gracious characteristics of Africa's children. The collective memory of ancestors who offered hospitality to Mary, Joseph, and the baby Jesus finds connection and expression in the hearts and souls of their descendants, especially at Christmastime.

So as we prepare for Christmas, I invite you on a journey. This journey begins with the birth and rescue of God's Son. Through scenarios drawn from my personal family history, you will come to know more about the people who offered hospitality to God's Son and whose descendants have been rescuing people ever since. Advent is a time for making new discoveries in light of God's revelation in the birth of Jesus Christ. I invite you to discover four disciplines that are ways of understanding and living out our call during the Christmas season. Christmas hospitality has to be cultivated by hard and deliberate effort; it is the fruit of the disciplined behavior of

1. Makin' Room
2. Makin' Do
3. Makin' Up, and
4. Makin' Time.

As we journey with a family of God's children, I share my family memories to help increase understanding of the true meaning of Christmas hospitality through an African American experience. May it empower us to be truly welcoming and inclusive of all God's children throughout the year!

Discipline One: Makin' Room

Purpose

To help students think about cultivating and living out hospitality between the diversity of God's people.

Prayer

Dear Lord, may the love you shower upon us during this season enlarge our spirits and our hearts, that we may in turn share the gift of Christian love with others. In Jesus' name. Amen.

An American Village

So Joseph also went up from the town of Nazareth in Galilee to Judea, to Bethlehem the town of David, because he belonged to the house and line of David. He went there to register with Mary, who was pledged to be married to him and was expecting a child. While they were there, the time came for the baby to be born, and she gave birth to her firstborn, a son. She wrapped him in cloths and placed him in a manger, because there was no room for them in the inn. (Luke 2:4-7, NIV)

*C*hristmas is a season of making room. As a child growing up, my grandparents' homes were the focal points of every holiday, major event, and activity. I grew up in a figurative village deep in the heart of Waco, Texas, a predominantly black community oddly named "White City," perhaps for the rows of white houses. I was surrounded by two sets of grandparents (who lived two blocks apart), uncles, aunts, and a host of cousins as well as close friends. I knew every family in my village.

Christmas was a fun time in the neighborhood. Relatives came from all over—Houston, Dallas, Fort Worth, Lubbock, Odessa and every other town in Central Texas, and from as far away as Denver, Colorado. The one thing we had to do was make room: room for Aunt Ruby and her family from Houston, Uncle JayArthur and his family from Lubbock, Uncle Riley and his clan from Odessa, Cousin Helen Ruth and those from the Dallas-Fort Worth area, Aunt Ezelma and our Great Migration clan from Denver and all those small towns in Central Texas—Satin, Chilton, Moorville, Marlin, Cameron, Lott, Rosebud, Robinson, Bellmead. We had to make room for lots of people. There were wall-to-wall people and nobody had the luxury of complaining. It would do no good, anyway!

The twenty-first-century world is a crowded place. With 6 billion people, cities are straining with sagging infrastructures. Los Angeles, California, where I live, is the second-largest city in America. Statistics

Population Statistics as of 2000

- Waco: 113,726 total; Whites: 60.8%; Blacks: 22.6%; Hispanic/Latino: 23.6%
- Houston: 1,953,631 total; Whites: 49.3%; Blacks: 25.3%; H/L: 37.4%
- Dallas: 1,188,580 total; Whites: 50.8%; Blacks: 25.9%; H/L: 35.6%
- Fort Worth: 534,694 total; Whites: 59.7%; Blacks: 25.9%; H/L: 35.6%
- Lubbock: 199,564 total; Whites: 72.9%; Blacks: 8.7%; H/L: 27.5%
- Odessa: 90,943 total; Whites: 73.4%; Blacks: 5.9%; H/L: 41.4%
- LA: 3,694,820 total; Whites: 46.7%; Blacks: 11.2%; Asian: 10%; H/L: 46.5%
- Denver: 554,636 total; Whites: 65.3%; Blacks: 11.1%; Asian: 2.8%; H/L: 31.7%

worldwide point to ever-burgeoning city populations. More people live in cities than ever before. More people live in my zip code than in my home-town of Waco, Texas, which boasted a population of 100,000 during my childhood. In Los Angeles, there are so many people, there is not room for them all. There are more homeless persons (80,000+) in Los Angeles than any other place in America. My city and most cities are not only larger, they are much more diverse as well. The size and changing demo-graphics make it complicated to share space. The different languages, cus-toms, and cultural nuances test our capacity to live together. Add the so-cial problems of gangs, high unem-ployment, limited or low income, and affordable housing, and our cities be-come not only crowded but difficult places in which to make room.

Racial/cultural tensions are em-phasized in crowded living quarters. Movies from *Remember the Titans* (2000, concerning the 1965 de-segregation of schools in Alexandria, Virginia) to *Crash* (2005, lifting up racial/ethnic tension and connection between Blacks/Whites/Mexicans/Persians/Koreans in Los Angeles) demonstrate the race consciousness of our postmodern world. Some soci-ologists and biblical scholars suggest that such a consciousness did not exist during biblical times or before the modern era. However, we know

Luke 10:25-37

The story that most peo-ple know as that of the good Samaritan only makes sense in terms of ethnicity and social status. The Sam-aritans were a mixed race people whose ancestry in-cluded the Hebrews of the Northern Kingdom and groups of conquered peo-ples brought in by the Assyr-ians. Jews, technically, were Hebrews descended from the tribe of Judah, whose geographical territory was in the Southern Kingdom. They became known as Jews during the Babylonian Exile, and, after the return, all who could count the ma-triarchal line as being He-brew (Ezra 9; 10; Nehemiah 13) were considered to be Jews. In this story, it is not only significant that a Sam-aritan, a person usually avoided by Jews of Jesus' time (John 4:7-9), is lifted up as the hero, it is also a criti-cal point to see that those of higher status in the Jewish community (the priestly class) chose not to be of help for one reason or an-other.

Mark 7:24-30

Even though Jesus told the Syrophoenician woman that he had come to the children first (the Jews), he was actually in her part of the world, having "gone away to the region of Tyre." Originally an island city in the Mediterranean Sea with territory close by on the coast, Tyre is now the fourth largest city in Lebanon. Tyre and Sidon were identified biblically as cities of Phoenicia. During the time of Jesus, this territory was designated as Syria, hence the woman identified was as Syrophoenician. Elijah had also found refuge in this region in Zarephath, which was situated north of Tyre and south of Sidon. The entire region is east and north of Galilee. Prophecy in Ezekiel 26–28 gives a great description of the Tyre of Old Testament times, revealing its importance to the region.

from stories like those of the good Samaritan (Luke 10:25-37) and Jesus and the Syrophoenician woman (Mark 7:24-30) that racial and cultural differences have caused tension throughout the ages. How do we make room in our hearts for one another?

The African Village

Then Joseph got up, took the child and his mother by night, and went to Egypt, and remained there until the death of Herod. This was to fulfill what had been spoken by the Lord through the prophet, "Out of Egypt I have called my son." (Matthew 2:14-15, NRSV)

The Bible reveals that the Hebrew people (known as Jews after the Babylonian Exile) had a checkered history in and with Egypt, a nation on the continent of Africa. Hebrew identity had a close relationship with African identity. Jesus' flight into Egypt retraces the flight of the ancient Hebrews into Egypt to escape famine (Genesis 45:4-11). It was by fleeing from Egypt that the Hebrew people became a covenant people, forming their identity. It is through the experience in Egypt that the children of Israel came into being as a nation. And certainly—as illustrated in the first name of the forty-fourth president of the United States, Barack Obama (*Barack* meaning "blessed" in Hebrew, Arabic, and Swahili)—Hebrew is an Afro-Asiatic language that is related to African languages from Kenya in East Africa to Chad and Mali in West Africa.

Hebrew is part of the family of languages known as the Afro-Asiatic grouping. There are 350 million speakers in the Afro-Asiatic family grouping and several subgroupings. Ancient Egyptian, biblical Hebrew, and Akkadian are included in the Afro-Asiatic language system.

- Cushitic/Omotic branch: Ethiopia, Eritrea, Djibouti, Somalia, Sudan, Kenya
- Berber: Tunisia, Mali, Chad, Libya, Mauritania, Algeria, Morocco, Egypt, Niger
- Chadic: Niger, Nigeria, Chad, Cameroon, Togo, Benin
- Semitic: Hebrew, Arabic, Ethiopic, Amharic
- Egyptian: Coptic (only used in the Coptic Church)

So Jesus is taken for protection to the place where his people were once in bondage and had to escape. Only God could make such a thing like this happen! What could the young Jewish family possibly find among Pharaoh's descendants? From the time of the Hebrew escape from Egypt, when "a mixed crowd also went up with them" (Exodus 12:38, NRSV), there had been centuries of interracial marriage between Hebrews and others, including Egyptians and Ethiopians.

While they were at Hazeroth, Miriam and Aaron spoke against Moses because of the Cushite woman whom he had married (for he had indeed married a Cushite woman). (Numbers 12:1, NRSV)

Do not abhor an Edomite, for he is your brother. Do not abhor an Egyptian, because you lived as an alien in his country. The third generation of children born to them may enter the assembly of the LORD. (Deuteronomy 23:7-8, NIV)

Now Elimelech, Naomi's husband, died, and she was left with her two sons. They married Moabite women, one named Orpah and the other Ruth. (Ruth 1:3-4a, NIV)

So Boaz took Ruth and she became his wife. Then he went to her, and the LORD enabled her to conceive, and she gave birth to a son. . . . And they named him Obed. He was the father of Jesse, the father of David. (Ruth 4:13, 17b, NIV)

Then David comforted his wife Bathsheba, and he went to her and lay with her. She gave birth to a son, and they named him Solomon. The LORD loved him. (2 Samuel 12:24, NIV)

Solomon made an alliance with Pharaoh king of Egypt and married his daughter. He brought her to the City of David. (1 Kings 3:1, NIV)

The Israelites are instructed not to abhor the Edomites or the Egyptians, for the Edomites are brothers (descended from Esau) and Egyptians may become members of Israel in their third generation. Naomi's Moabite daughter-in-law, Ruth, marries Boaz and gives birth to Obed, the grandfather of David. David falls in love with and kills for Bathsheba, whose name means "daughter of the oath," "seventh daughter," or "daughter of Sheba." They have a son, Solomon, who is visited by the Queen of Sheba (1 Kings 10) and who marries an Egyptian princess. Sheba was a kingdom that spanned from southern Arabia into the Horn of Africa, inclusive of Yemen, Ethiopia/Cush, Somalia, Eritrea, and Djibouti. Parts of Ethiopia and Sudan were considered to be Upper Egypt. It is from this lineage that Jesus was born.

So perhaps Joseph, Mary, and the baby Jesus were more "at home" in Egypt than previously imagined or reported by biblical historians, commentators, and interpreters. Further, these factors and the similarity of the ancient sociological/family structure to much of Africa are reasons that modern-day Africans and much of the African Diaspora are so "at home" in the Bible. Perhaps a greater truth is that the Bible was more at home in Africa. Nevertheless, Jesus spent his early days of existence on African soil, a land of natural wonders and generous people. Convinced that Herod's threat was real, Jesus' parents took the well-traveled route to Egypt in Africa as a means of escape. Perhaps there was something in the African village where they took refuge that resonated with their sense of belonging and belief system and values.

Even more significant were the values of that African/Egyptian village that made them a people defined more by their hospitality—expressed in the concept of *ubuntu*—than their hostility. Nobel Peace Prize winner Desmond Tutu is a strong advocate of this practice (*ubuntu*) of Africans sharing with others—in their villages, towns, and around the world. Through African feasts and celebrations, villagers come together to offer mutual support resources.

In our African understanding, part of Ubantu—being human—is the rare gift of sharing. This concept of sharing is exemplified at African feasts . . . when people eat together from a common dish. . . . That means a meal is indeed to have communion with one's fellows. . . . So I would look for a socio-economic system that placed the emphasis on sharing and giving rather than on self-aggrandisement and getting.[1]

Figures on Church Growth

The United Methodist Church in West Africa has grown over 400% in the last ten years. As of early 2010, 35.4% of United Methodists lived outside the United States: 32.5% in Africa, 2% in Asia, and .9% in Europe. The dominant language of Christianity is Spanish. At current growth rates, by 2025 more Christians of any denomination will live in Africa and in Latin America than anywhere else in the world.

Africans have always been a giving, sharing people, even those carried away in chains. Perhaps this nature has been advantageous to opportunists and persons of ill will. Africans and Native Americans have experienced as truth this saying: "When the white man (missionaries) came, he had his Bible, we had our land. He asked us to pray. When our eyes were opened, we had his Bible and he had our land."

Despite the lost, stolen, and strayed history of black people, they have forged new chapters of survival, nestled in communities that kept on giving and reaching out. God admonished the Israelites when they left Egypt that God "loves the strangers, providing them food and clothing." They were instructed do likewise (Deuteronomy 10:18-19, NRSV).

The fact that Christianity is growing rapidly on the African continent while in decline in Europe and the West is illustrative of the affection and solidarity Africans have with the person of Jesus Christ. The powerful Gospel stories and the courage and compassion of Jesus spoke and speak to these people of the "darker hue."

It may be that black people are so "at home" in the Bible because the God they came to know in Jesus resonated with their own innate spirit of kindness and giving. It was only natural for that Egyptian village to welcome Joseph and Mary and the sweet little Jesus boy, a boy who grew up to be the man who told us to be perfect in love, including even to those who persecute us (Matthew 5:43-48).

17

The Village of God's Kingdom

In my Father's house are many rooms; if it were not so, I would have told you. I am going there to prepare a place for you. (John 14:2, NIV)

Reflecting on the village places of my growing-up years, I see the linkage with my ancestral roots. The values of my family and community had roots in an ancestry of extended hospitality that emanated from our Lord Jesus Christ himself. (Say "Amen," somebody!) Jesus was always makin' room for somebody, especially when no one else would.

- He made room for children when his own disciples were unwelcoming. (Luke 18:15-17)
- He made room for sick people when others had given up. (John 5:1-9; Luke 8:40-56)
- He made room for poor people while others looked down on them. (Luke 16:19-22)
- He made room for women in a world that ignored them. (Luke 7:36-50)
- He made room for people of a different ethnicity and culture. (John 4:7-10)
- He made room for rich people whom others disdained. (John 3:1-3)
- He made room for sinners who had lost their way. (Luke 23:39-43)
- He made room for his own adversaries. "Father forgive them!" he cried, while he was being crucified. (Luke 23:33-34)

Being a Christian is about makin' room. In celebrating the birth of Jesus, we are reminded that God made room for us and we are to make room for others. Yes, that includes the chronically drunk uncle, the sleeping-around cousin, the drug-addict brother, the parolee friend, the showing-off neighbor, the dressed-for-success companion of the first cousin, the get-along-with-nobody aunt, and a host of others only you can name that show up at large family gatherings like Christmas.

As we move out from our villages of origin, we discover that we must enlarge our circle of inclusion, makin' room for more and more folk. Upon entering school, I had to make room for people who were different from me. In Waco, there were only two high schools for people of African American descent; we had to make room for people who came from different parts of town. For a season, I lived in Denver, Colorado with a cousin who only had girls and wanted the experience of having a son. There I had to make room for people who talked differently and who had different customs. Segregated Waco was another world from Denver, where Whites and Blacks actually dated one another. After a year, I returned home to Waco and enrolled in Paul Quinn College, a historically black college.[2] There I had to make room for classmates from other places like Yazoo, Mississippi, Mobile, Alabama, and Slidell, Louisiana.

During college, I responded to a call to ministry, and immediately after graduation I left for seminary at Perkins School of Theology at Southern Methodist University in Dallas, Texas. Again, another world! I had to make room not only for living and attending class with white people on a regular basis, but also for people of different Christian denominations, non-Christians, atheists, seekers, and women going into ministry! When I graduated and began to pastor, I had to make room for other persons' ideas about how to "run the church" and the radical elements in the inner city demanding change in our church and governmental systems. And when I got married, I had to make room for someone else sharing my space—permanently!

When we had children and started our own Christmas rituals, we resurrected the values of my childhood village at my in-laws' and my oldest sister's house. Here, we gather again to make room for the families. It is incredible how what was done for Joseph and his family in the Egyptian village just keeps repeating itself in my life. What that African village did in welcoming the Holy Family safeguarded the promise God had delivered to the world. The birth of Jesus was God's incarnate sign of the promise that God was indeed makin' room for all families, no matter the color, class, culture, or ethnicity, to be included in the kingdom of God through Jesus Christ. There is plenty good room in the Father's kingdom.

Advent is a season of makin' room. How do we make room in our hearts for the strangers among us, who have no place to go and no one to whom they can turn? We have a rich culture on which to draw in learning to accept all of humanity as our brothers and sisters. By calling up our African roots and practicing *ubuntu*, as did that ancient village in Egypt to which Joseph and Mary fled with the young child, Jesus, we can know how to make room. By practicing the love that Jesus demonstrated in his life and in the stories he told, we can know how to make room. After telling the parable of the good Samaritan, Jesus said, "Go and do likewise." May we heed his call today, as we enter this Advent season.

NOTES

1. Desmond Tutu, *Crying in the Wilderness: The Struggle for Justice in South Africa* (Grand Rapids: Eerdmans, 1990), 100.
2. An AME-affiliated school, Paul Quinn College moved to Dallas in 1990, occupying the former campus of Bishop College, a Baptist-affiliated school that closed its doors in 1988.

Discipline Two: Makin' Do

Purpose

To help students experience Advent from the perspective of "makin' do," which is about trusting God as compared to trusting in wealth.

Prayer

Dear Lord God, we thank you for always being sufficient for our every need. Help us to be like Paul, knowing that although we may be in need, we can live as though we have plenty. We ask this in the precious name of Jesus, our Christ. Amen.

Jesus Was Poor

After eight days had passed, it was time to circumcise the child; and he was called Jesus, the name given by the angel before he was conceived in the womb. When the time came for their purification according to the law of Moses, they brought him up to Jerusalem to present him to the Lord (as it is written in the law of the Lord, "Every firstborn male shall be designated as holy to the Lord"), and they offered a sacrifice according to what is stated in the law of the Lord, "a pair of turtledoves or two young pigeons." (Luke 2:21-24, NRSV)

C hristmas is a season of "makin' do." Time is closing in on preparations for Christmas; there is no more time to save money for gifts and groceries. It is time to use what you have. Mary and Joseph made do. Mary was probably very young when she gave birth to Jesus, as young as thirteen or fourteen years old. Given the historical time and conditions, young women married very early. As a "young virgin," she was highly favored by God, despite her lowly estate as a female and a peasant. In her visit to Elizabeth she said, "My soul magnifies the Lord, and my spirit rejoices in God my Savior, for he has looked with favor on the lowliness of his servant" (Luke 1:47-48). Upon the birth of Jesus, Mary and Joseph were obliged to follow the custom of Jewish families regarding childbirth ceremonies. According to the law of Moses, the mother must bring to the priest a lamb less than a year old for a burnt offering and a pigeon or a turtledove for a sin offering.

> When the days of her purification are completed, whether for a son or for a daughter, she shall bring to the priest at the entrance of the tent of meeting a lamb in its first year for a burnt offering, and a pigeon or a turtledove for a sin offering. . . . If she cannot afford a sheep, she shall take two turtledoves or two pigeons, one for the burnt offering and the other for a sin offering; and the priest shall make atonement on her behalf, and she shall be clean. (Leviticus 12:6, 8, NRSV)

In his book *Jesus and the Disinherited,* Howard Thurman[1] elaborates on the social and theological significance of our Scripture lesson. He explains that Jesus was not only a Jew; he was a poor Jew. The fact that his parents could not afford a lamb, forcing them to settle for a substitute offering of two doves, clearly demonstrated their dire economic straits. Being born poor placed Jesus among the great masses of people on the earth—then and now. Again God acts in a way that reveals God's power in paradox: royalty is placed in a barn full of smelly animals. In birth, Jesus is in solidarity with not only the vast number of his people, but also with the great company of people in the world.

Is it any wonder that Christianity is experiencing such tremendous growth in countries where poverty is rampant, yet struggling to survive among the industrialized, wealthy, and privileged countries of the Western world? Just as Jesus identified with the poor in his day, Jesus still identifies with the masses of people in the world who are poor. Jesus'

**Children's Defense Fund Figures
on Childhood Poverty, Early 2010**

- 14.1 million children in America are poor, including 1.5 million infants and toddlers
- 1 out of 3 is black
- 3 out of 10 are Latino
- 1 out of 11 is white
- 6.3 million children live in families with an income below $11,035 for a family of four

(Established by Marian Wright Edelman in 1973, the Children's Defense Fund has been "leading our nation to ensure a level playing field for all children.")

pronouncement that "you always have the poor with you" (Matthew 26:11, NRSV) was just as much a prediction as a statement of fact. It certainly was not his or his Father's desire! The same condition that made people poor in Jesus' time persists to this day: the desire for and misuse of power and wealth. The masses were drawn to Jesus then and now because he was anointed to bring God's message to the poor (Luke 4:18). Mary and Joseph did what most poor families who struggle to survive do: they made do.

A Hand-Me-Down Society

"The Spirit of the Lord is upon me, because he has anointed me to bring good news to the poor. He has sent me to proclaim release to the captives and recovery of sight to the blind, to let the oppressed go free, to proclaim the year of the Lord's favor." (Luke 4:18-19, NRSV)

Like many, I grew up in a village of caring, loving, protective people. My parents, however, were not high school graduates. From an economic standpoint, they could not afford to buy new Christmas presents for their six children. Anything new was very inexpensive. And then there were the gifts that were new to us. My first bicycle was bought from the secondhand store on Elm in East Waco. It was not brand-new,

What Does the Bible Say About How the Poor Are to Be Treated?

When you reap the harvest of your land, you shall not reap to the very edges of your field, or gather the gleanings of your harvest. You shall not strip your vineyard bare, or gather the fallen grapes of your vineyard; you shall leave them for the poor and the alien: I am the LORD your God.   (Leviticus 19:9-10, NRSV)

There will, however, be no one in need among you, because the LORD is sure to bless you in the land that the LORD your God is giving you as a possession to occupy, if only you will obey the LORD your God by diligently observing this entire commandment that I command you today.   (Deuteronomy 15:4-5, NRSV)

If there is among you anyone in need, a member of your community in any of your towns within the land that the LORD your God is giving you, do not be hard-hearted or tight-fisted toward your needy neighbor. You should rather open your hand . . .
                    (Deuteronomy 15:7-8, NRSV)

Give justice to the weak and the orphan;
    maintain the right of the lowly and the destitute.
Rescue the weak and the needy;
    deliver them from the hand of the wicked.
                    (Psalm 82:3-4, NRSV)

It is you who have devoured the vineyard;
    the spoil of the poor is in your houses.
What do you mean by crushing my people,
    by grinding the face of the poor? says the Lord GOD of hosts.
                    (Isaiah 3:14b-15, NRSV)

Thus says the LORD:
For three transgressions of Israel,
    and for four, I will not revoke the punishment;
because they sell the righteous for silver,
    and the needy for a pair of sandals—
they who trample the head of the poor into the dust of the earth,
    and push the afflicted out of the way.   (Amos 2:6-7a, NRSV)

but it was new to me and that is what mattered. While many families, regardless of ethnicity, have faced economic challenges, when black families are forced to rely on secondhand stuff and hand-me-downs, it is a reminder of the history of second-class citizenship that black Americans had to endure for so long:

- Hand-me-down-clothes
- Hand-me-down textbooks
- Hand-me-down athletic equipment
- Hand-me-down houses
- Hand-me-down school buildings.

Despite the fact that their families paid the same taxes as others, black children had to use outdated textbooks, athletic equipment, and even school buildings passed down from white institutions. But we made do; we learned anyway! When Thurgood Marshall, the first African American to serve on the U.S. Supreme Court, was giving his remarks at his retirement, he was asked, "Mr. Supreme Court Justice, what would you like written on your tombstone?" He replied, "He did what he could with what he had."

The history of black people in America and around the world bespeaks Justice Marshall's solemn yet eloquent words. For Africa's descendants and many others have always had to "make do" with what they had and make the best of bad situations. In a previous publication I wrote:

> One of my early Christian teachers often said, "Do your best and leave to God the rest." The wonderfully exciting thing about the God we serve is that God takes care of "the rest" in ways that yet confound and overwhelm us. What God has done in the stories of Moses, Joseph, Daniel, Esther, Rahab, Paul, Mary Magdalene, he also did in Simon—took a bad situation and turned it into something good for the kingdom.[2]

There are times when we all must "make do" with situations and circumstances as they present themselves in our lives. Sometimes, "It is what it is," for even God has to deal with the circumstances of our lives. In fact, the Incarnation—God coming in the flesh—is God's response to our circumstances. It helps to remember that this is why Jesus came—to bring good news to the poor and healing for those who suffer. Thus, the Advent and Christmas season is a time to celebrate how God chose to become involved in the messiness of human existence.

The Genius of Survival

Now after they had left, an angel of the Lord appeared to Joseph in a dream and said, "Get up, take the child and his mother, and flee to Egypt, and remain there until I tell you; for Herod is about to search for the child, to destroy him." (Matthew 2:13, NRSV)

But the more they were oppressed, the more they multiplied and spread, so that the Egyptians came to dread the Israelites. (Exodus 1:12, NRSV)

There is nothing messier in human existence than a condition of terrorism, slavery, and oppression. That Jesus and his family found liberation in the land where their ancestors had been enslaved is a reversal of the deliverance story that symbolizes God's redeeming power. At the same time, baby Jesus' need for flight into Egypt has its parallel in the Hebrew need for flight from Egypt. In the first and second chapters of Exodus, the story is told about how Pharaoh and the Egyptians feel threatened by the enormous growth of the enslaved Hebrews. To remedy the situation, Pharaoh imposes population control measures. He tries to overwork the Hebrew men to make them less sexually active. Failing this, he gives orders to the Hebrew midwives to murder all Hebrew male newborns. When this did not work, Pharaoh sent his soldiers to slay all the Hebrew boys.

During this time, a Levite woman, Jochebed, had a son. She managed to hide him for three months. For fear of having him discovered and executed by Pharaoh, Jochebed put her baby boy in a basket and hid him among the reeds while her daughter Miriam watched. Having little recourse, Jochebed had to make do with the circumstances at hand. In the end, having been discovered by Pharaoh's daughter and raised up in the royal palace, the boy, who was meant for destruction, becomes the liberator of the Hebrews.

God can make something out of nothing, and God empowers people not only to make do but also to flourish. You may have heard the saying, "Life is only 10 percent of how you make it and 90 percent of how you take it." This certainly applies to the African experience in the world and to their descendants in North America. As Africans were bought and brought to America to be sold as slaves, they were faced with an enormous burden they did not create. Thus, they had to "make do" with an extremely horrible situation. The ability to thrive despite centuries of captivity and endangerment became known as the "genius of survival." Why "genius"? I attended a lecture at Southern Methodist University in 1970, in which Dr. Lerone Bennett[3] explained that the most remarkable thing about the slaves' voyage to America was not how many had died but how many survived. The seeds of survival genius were sown in the choppy waters of the transatlantic slave trade.

Over and over, the slaves' will to survive would be tested by slave masters and inhuman conditions. Though sold as chattel property, stripped of their language, and robbed of their heritage, the African slaves would beat back the forces of dehumanization and environmental death chambers (cotton fields) to create ways of speaking, literature, and music that continue to influence and enrich the entire world. Against the onslaught of slavery and oppression, segregation, discrimination, Jim Crow laws and color and class indignity, and racism in the United States and apartheid in South Africa, they mounted a fight for freedom and restoration of their human dignity that continues.

The genius of survival is evidenced by the body of literary work left from the Harlem Renaissance and by the way the slaves and their descendants used the weapons intended for their domestication—

The Harlem Renaissance was more than a literary movement. Its focus was on racial consciousness and justice as led by W. E. B. DuBois and the "back to Africa" movement led by Marcus Garvey, as well as the appreciation of jazz, spirituals and blues, the visual arts, and dramatic revues. In his influential book *The New Negro* (1925), Alain Locke, professor at Howard University, described the movement as "something like a spiritual emancipation." Writers and artists included: Zora Neale Hurston, Langston Hughes, James Weldon Johnson, Arna Bontemps, Aaron Douglass, R. Rosamond Johnson, Lois Mailou Jones, and Duke Ellington.

27

Christian theology and the Bible—as the very instruments to set them free. "Slaves, obey your earthly masters with respect and fear, and with sincerity of heart" (Ephesians 6:5, NIV). With Scriptures such as this one, the slave masters tried to use Christianity as the very means to make the slaves docile and fully accepting of their slave status. Theologian and mystic Howard Thurman often recounted how his grandmother would ask him to read her anything from the Bible except Paul's writings. The teachings found in certain Pauline passages were not consonant with what she understood about God.

The slaves and slave descendants, being true to their genius, took the same Jesus that the slave master tried to use against them to find Jesus, the champion and example of freedom. They looked to the Bible, the weapon intended for their domesticated existence, and found in it the words and personalities to help set them free. In the Bible, they found a people who learned to "make do" with what they had while trusting in a liberating God who would take what others meant for harm and make it into something good. As Joseph said to his brothers, "Even though you intended to do harm to me, God intended it for good, in order to preserve a numerous people, as he is doing today" (Genesis 50:20, NRSV).

Our Situation Versus God's Destination

> And the child's father and mother were amazed at what was being said about him. Then Simeon blessed them and said to his mother Mary, "This child is destined for the falling and the rising of many in Israel, and to be a sign that will be opposed so that the inner thoughts of many will be revealed—and a sword will pierce your own soul too." (Luke 2:33-35, NRSV)

Joseph and Mary had "a situation" in their lives with which they had to deal. It could not be wished or prayed away. Such is life—even for Christians. We all have things come up. Bad things happen to good people, even the Holy Family. Their story reminds us to make do with what we have or what we are presented. Quoting his mother, Oscar-winning actor Denzel Washington said, "Life comes down to four things: the grace of God, the will of God, the hand you're dealt and the way you play it." Like the apostle Paul, we must learn to be content with all things.

I am not saying this because I am in need, for I have learned to be content whatever the circumstances. (Philippians 4:11, NIV)

We need to get beyond thinking that Christmas is spoiled if you can't buy gifts for everyone in your family or circle of friends. When Jesus was presented for circumcision at the Temple on the eighth day as prescribed by the law, his parents offered as a sacrifice two young pigeons, the gift allowed for those who could not afford to bring a lamb. Mary and Joseph were makin' do! Like them, we should "do our best and trust God to do the rest." When the Pharaohs of this world try to create situations and circumstances to blunt your future and interfere with your destiny, make do with what you have. When the Herods of the world try to deny you space and place, make do with what you have. God will make a way. That is the biblical record and the testimony of the ancestors.

The "genius of survival" continues to be a strength for many African American families. It has been portrayed on film and in reality. In her role as a single black mother raising children in Tyler Perry's movie *Meet the Browns*, Angela Bassett speaks a great truth: "One thing a black woman knows how to do, is how to 'make it.'" In a 2008 CNN series titled *Black America*, a young single father with two children living in New York City is featured. The ten-year-old son is a gifted student; however, the family has moved frequently, causing the children to attend five different schools. In this episode, the family is threatened with eviction because the landlord wants to convert his property into more profitable purposes. As a result, they must move again. This devoted father is committed to "weathering the storm" as he tries to survive on a part-time job and a government subsidy from Social Security. When asked by the CNN reporter how long he would survive, the father insists, "We just have to make do 'til times get better."

On any given night in America, up to 2 million people are homeless. According to the report of the U.S. Conference of Mayors (2000):
- 50% are African American
- 35% are white
- 12% are Hispanic
- 2% are Native American
- 1% are Asian
- 44% are single men
- 12% are single women
- 36% are families with children
- 7% are unaccompanied minors

Angels and Friends

This New Yorker represents a continuum of the African American experience celebrated throughout life and coming to full expression at Christmas. Black folk in many families keep finding a way to celebrate Christmas with a "make do" spirit. As we open up our homes and our lives to relatives, friends, and strangers, we'll find that menus designed to feed ten people will satisfy fifty. Mary and Joseph were faced with a terrible situation: a young couple with a child and nowhere to go. And to make matters worse, they drew the ire of Herod because their child was special. God intervened and sent an angel and a village of friends. When we make do with our bad situations, God sends us angels and friends. As this Christmas approaches, think about all the times and places God sent you angels and friends. And particularly try to remind yourself of those Christmas seasons in which you needed angels and friends more than you needed some material gift!

As you celebrate the angels and friends God sends to you and the villages God sends you to, perhaps you will be motivated to offer someone else hospitality this Advent season. Become an angel and bring a message of hope to someone on the edge. Be a friend indeed to a friend in need. Offer your household as a village, a place of refuge and caring. At its deepest level, this is what the season is all about: the gift of hospitality! If we take the focus off getting and place it on giving, we will discover or rediscover the truer meaning of the season. In so doing, a new generation will learn not to be disappointed when "It is what it is." Let us all be grateful for what it is because the best gifts are the offerings of our selves and our spirits. Create a "make do" Christmas for you and yours!

NOTES

1. Howard Thurman (d. 1981), black mystic and theologian, served at Howard, Boston, Morehouse, and Spelman. He wrote more than twenty books.

2. Henry L. Masters, Sr., *Simon of Cyrene: The Crossbearer of Jesus Who Was the Only African Eyewitness to the Crucifixion* (Portland, OR: Inkwater Press, 2004), 65-66.

3. Dr. Lerone Bennett, Jr., scholar, author, and social historian, was the executive editor of *Ebony Magazine* for fifty years, contributing many essays on African American history. He also wrote *Before the Mayflower: A History of Black America 1619–1962* and *Forced Into Glory: Abraham Lincoln's White Dream.*

Discipline Three: Makin' Up

Purpose

To help students come to understand the concept of forgiveness and reconnection, especially in the season of Advent.

Prayer

Dear God, thank you for your forgiveness. Help us to honor you by having an attitude of forgiveness toward family and community during this season of Advent. In the matchless name of Jesus, the baby of the manger. Amen.

Reunion

After Herod died, an angel of the Lord appeared in a dream to Joseph in Egypt and said, "Get up, take the child and his mother and go to the land of Israel, for those who were trying to take the child's life are dead." So he got up, took the child and his mother and went to the land of Israel. (Matthew 2:19-21, NIV)

*C*hristmas is a time of makin' up, a time of reunion and reconciliation. It is a time when families agree to bury the hatchet carried
against long-lost, wandering-sheep family members and make up.
Upon receiving word from an angel that it was safe, Joseph and Mary
took their child and went back home. Though they had been received
with open arms and treated well by their Egyptian village, they wanted
to go back home. Most people who leave home have an innate desire, a
spiritual longing, to go back home. They want to be able to go back!
While some leave home in a good way, there are many who leave home
in a bad way. When one leaves in a bad way, hurriedly, secretly, as did
Joseph and Mary, in the midst of scandal or bad behavior, it often requires some makin' up in order to go back home.

My parents had separated and divorced by the time I was in first
grade. My dad, who had been considered "a good black man," just decided to walk away from our family, which included my mom and five
children. I was the youngest and deeply impacted. It was a painful time.
I begged my mother to help me understand why. My father became a
persona non grata in our small, close-knit community. How could he just
walk away from his wife and all those children? Even my paternal grandparents, with whom I was very close, had few kind words for their son's
behavior. In a few years my father relocated and, at the insistence of my
paternal grandmother, reconnected with my family. No one really wanted
much to do with him, except me. As a nine-year-old boy, I longed to be
with my dad under any circumstance. The family made arrangements
for me to spend summers and holidays with my dad. Of those times,
Christmas was the most memorable.

My dad lived in Rosebud, Texas, a whopping thirty-six miles from my
hometown of Waco. The best-known accomplishment of this town of
1,200 is that of being the birthplace of LaDainian Tomlinson, a running
back who came into the National Football League in 2001. In preparation
for my visit, my mom would take me to the Circle, a popular intersection
in south Waco, where I would wait for my dad, who worked construction
jobs and often came through Waco. I remember the waiting. I was anx-
ious to see and be with my dad. When he arrived I would get in the car-
load of construction workers, crawl over musky, beer-drinking bodies,
and land in the lap of my dad! We then drove to his house for the Christmas holidays.

At the moment I landed in his lap, all was right with me in my world. Many in the community, including myself, had hard feelings against my father. But now all was forgiven, the hatchet was buried, as he and I would spend time "makin' up." We would go to the ice cream store for a special treat—just me and my dad. Like any child, I was full of unconditional love for my father during these special times. Children are so trusting and forgiving and so full of unconditional love, the basis for forgiveness. This is why they were so drawn to Jesus, and he to them, during his lifetime. One story tells of a young girl who was reprimanded by her father, "Now just remember that I love you and I especially love you when you obey and do good." He expressed his love conditionally. Nevertheless the daughter replied, "Oh, thank you, Daddy, but I love you *all* the time." She expressed her love unconditionally. Indeed, forgiveness and unconditional love are at the core of Jesus' teaching.

Forgiveness

"You have heard that it was said, 'Love your neighbor and hate your enemy.' But I tell you: Love your enemies and pray for those who persecute you, that you may be sons of your Father in heaven. He causes his sun to rise on the evil and the good, and sends rain on the righteous and the unrighteous. If you love those who love you, what reward will you get? Are not even the tax collectors doing that? And if you greet only your brothers, what are you doing more than others? Do not even pagans do that? Be perfect, therefore, as your heavenly Father is perfect." (Matthew 5:43-48, NIV)

Forgiveness makes it possible for us to experience the true gifts of the Advent and Christmas seasons. For God so loved us that he gave Jesus Christ. God offers forgiveness through Jesus Christ. Despite our willful disobedience, our flirtation with other gods, our groping in the dark for suitable answers to our human problems, and our killing of prophets, God chose to offer his Son as a sin offering and reconciling gift to a broken humanity. Jesus taught forgiveness in a parable about a wayward son and a generous father (Luke 15:11-32). He taught forgiveness as an object lesson at the time of his arrest (Matthew 26:50-52). From his Sermon on the Mount (Matthew 5:43-48) to his crucifixion (Luke 23:34), when the dying Savior pronounced mercy on those who were killing him, forgiveness was a core value of Jesus' teachings. It is so central to the Christian life that Jesus included it in the prayer he taught, which Christians have prayed for over two millennia: "and forgive us our debts, as we also have forgiven our debtors" (Matthew 6:12, NRSV).

Forgiveness made it possible for my father and me to experience reunion and continue life together. I made new friends in Rosebud and had an alternate family system. I looked forward to seeing and being with them at Christmas and in the summer. These people were part of a scrapbook of my childhood life; they also represent lifelong relationships. Forgiveness is what enables me to have the memories of my father's house on the gravel road, of his twin stepsons who treated me like a little brother, and of helping my dad string Christmas lights.

Forgiveness is what enabled otherwise ostracized and estranged cousins and relatives the opportunity to come back home for Christmas. At Christmas, a special effort was made to contact and invite these family members. No matter what the infraction, the sin, the difference, or the offense, everybody was always welcome to my grandparents' home for Christmas. The alcoholic uncle, the banished son-in-law, the promiscuous aunt, the heathen grandchildren, the lying daughter, the homosexual first cousin, the snobbish, well-to-do nephew from upstate: everyone was welcome at Christmastime.

The embrace of the forgiveness ethos continued in the holiday traditions practiced in my adult life. Every Christmas my wife and I would first take the children to see my dad and my mom, even though we spent the majority of the holiday season with her side of the family. Gifts are provided for persons who may be considered *persona non grata*, for those who may just show up unannounced, and for the unexpected stranger. After all, it's Christmas, and everyone is implored to have the Christmas spirit. The Christmas spirit is a spirit of forgiveness that empowers us to reach out to others who may be different, may have "issues," or may have nowhere else to go. We bring them into our gift-giving time, invite them to the parties and to church, and help them feel the power and grace of our incarnate Lord made real in us.

We are not flawless; we are fallen and forgiven. This forgiveness finds its expression in the gift of a Savior who comes to a sinful humanity and offers redemptive love. Just as God came to set us free from sin, we are more completely free ourselves when we love one another. As the hymn writer penned:

> Love came down at Christmas,
> Love, all lovely, Love divine;
> Love was born at Christmas;
> Stars and angels gave the sign.
>   Christina G. Rossetti (*The United Methodist Hymnal*, 242)

Back Home

The Holy Family, Mary, Joseph, and Jesus, went back home, not looking for vengeance or retaliation but allowing God to continue the plan and purpose God had for their lives. God's plans are greater than those of earthly rulers like Herod. It was true then and is true now. It was true for Joseph, Mary, and Jesus, and it's true for you. We must be able to let go of some things in life if we want God to help us reach our goals and fulfill our purpose. Advent is a time to remember what Dr. King so eloquently said: "I can never be what I ought to be until you are what you ought to be, and you can never be what you ought to be until I am what I ought to be."[1] None of us can be our true selves in God without recognizing the dignity in each other.

The belief that community brings out our best selves is deeply woven into the fabric of African ways of being, of ubuntu. To experience "shared community" requires acceptance of others without regard to differences. African teaching and culture is reflected in its proverbs:

- Talking to one another is loving one another.
- Let your love be like the misty rain, coming softly, but flooding the river. (Madagascar)
- If relatives help each other, what evil can hurt them? (Ethiopia)
- A flame burns best when it is passed on.
- When the ax entered the forest, the tree said, "The handle is one of us." (Nigeria)
- One tree, receiving all the wind, breaks.
- A river is filled by its tributaries.
- Love me as you do cotton; add to the thin and rejoin the broken.
- Through others I am somebody. (South Africa)

35

Behind and beyond African proverbs is a solid foundation of Christian thought as formed and fashioned in the theological expression of North African church fathers, especially Augustine. Augustine (354–430) is respected in the all branches of the church, Catholic, Orthodox, and Protestant. Born and educated in North Africa, as a young man he was thoroughly immoral, a womanizer and a rabble-rouser. His mother, Monica, never stopped praying for him. Who knows better than Augustine what the power of forgiveness can do? After his conversion, Augustine gave us that immortal thought in the opening paragraph of his *Confessions:* "Thou, O Lord, has made us for thyself, and our souls are restless until they find rest in thee." His writings, which include *City of God* and *Confessions*, shaped Christian thinking about the nature of sin and evil, free will, and the Trinity.

Augustine was a Berber, a people native to Africa. North African scholarship came from the same region of the world and cultural environment where the Holy Family took refuge. Out of Africa the Holy Family came; out of Africa came the theological foundation for the early church. It is significant that, just as African hospitality disciplines required acceptance of this family, Christian discipleship finds ultimate meaning and application in receiving the theological reality of Jesus Christ as Savior, Master, and Lord.

Makin' Up Is Hard to Do

Sometimes we, like Jesus, have to leave home. For him, it was to escape danger. For the prodigal son (Luke 15:11-32), it was his fascination with bright lights and the big city.

James Weldon Johnson (1871–1938) was a prominent figure of the Harlem Renaissance. He was a lawyer, professor at Fisk University, songwriter, and the first field secretary and executive secretary of the NAACP. In 1927, he published *God's Trombones: Seven Negro Sermons in Verse,* a collection that demonstrated the lyrical, oratory giftedness of the black preacher. In "The Prodigal Son," Johnson paints a picture of the place to which the "young man" of Luke 15 traveled: ". . . at night-time he came to a city. / And the city was bright in the night-time like day . . ."[2]

For Ruth, it was to go with Naomi and find a better life. For the enslaved African and the exiled Jew, it was by force. Whether one leaves voluntarily or by force, there is still the longing to return home, as expressed in Psalm 137:1-5.

> By the rivers of Babylon we sat and wept
>   when we remembered Zion.
> There on the poplars
>   we hung our harps,
> for there our captors asked us for songs,
>   our tormentors demanded songs of joy;
>   they said, "Sing us one of the songs of Zion!"
> How can we sing the songs of the LORD
>   while in a foreign land?
> If I forget you, O Jerusalem,
>   may my right hand forget its skill.
>   (Psalm 137:1-5, NIV)

The last verses of the psalm show that, often, making up is hard to do. The exiled Jews wanted revenge and payback.

> Remember, O LORD, what the Edomites did on the day Jerusalem fell.
>   "Tear it down," they cried, "tear it down to its foundations!"
> O Daughter of Babylon, doomed to destruction,
>   happy is he who repays you for what you have done to us—
> he who seizes your infants and dashes them against the rocks.
>   (Psalm 137:7-9, NIV)

Forgiveness is the means through which we must make the reentry home. As God provided a way for Jesus and his family to return home, God also provides a way for all of us to return home. What better time can this return be made than Christmas? It is the season of Advent, a time for "new beginnings." It is a time for letting go of things in the past: grudges, insults, offenses, hurt feelings, abuses, mistreatments, and so on. If we don't let go, we will be like the monkey with his hands in the jar—unable to get away because he won't let go of the goods he is holding.

Perhaps there is someone you need to forgive and let back into your life. Let this Christmas be the time to allow God to work another miracle through you. Just as Mary made herself available for God to use to bring his Son into the world, ask God to use you to help bring transformation to someone who needs love and forgiveness. The offer of these gifts will create the best Christmas ever for you, for them, and for all in the community. As Nike says, "Just do it!" You will be amazed at the power of forgiveness. Lost family members can be reclaimed by this power. Enemies can be reconciled, adversaries can be reunited, nations can find peace, and sinners will be redeemed. God's power is so amazing. It is only by God's power that makin' up is possible. And yet it is the cornerstone of the Christmas story.

> The wolf will live with the lamb, the leopard will lie down with the goat,
> the calf and the lion and the yearling together;
> and a little child will lead them.
> The cow will feed with the bear, their young will lie down together,
> and the lion will eat straw like the ox.
> The infant will play near the hole of the cobra,
> and the young child put his hand into the viper's nest.
> They will neither harm nor destroy on all my holy mountain,
> for the earth will be full of the knowledge of the LORD as the
> waters cover the sea.
>
> (Isaiah 11:6-9, NIV)

It is no longer "business as usual." Through the gift of a baby boy, the powers of the world are radically altered. The last is first (Matthew 20:16); the poor have good news preached to them; the blind recover sight; liberty is proclaimed; and the oppressed are set free (Luke 4:18). No wonder Jesus was a threat to Herod and the Holy Family had to flee! Jesus was and is a threat to all who seek to exclude people from the blessings of God on the basis of their race, color, gender, socioeconomic status, or even past sins. And yet, even family systems have power structures with rules about who belongs and who does not. However, Jesus came for the same people for whom he would later die. The Scripture passage John 3:16 lets us know that Jesus came for "whoever" (NIV) and "everyone" (NRSV)! Christmas should be the most inclusive time of the year, as demonstrated by my grandparents. All were welcomed in my grandparents' homes; all were welcome in my in-laws' home; and now, all are welcome in my home. You too may have relatives who exemplify the gift of hospitality, the discipline of "makin' up." Look around this Advent season and see if there is someone you need to reach out to and practice genuine yuletide hospitality.

The Power of Makin' Up

The power of makin' up can bring joy to the world for many people who suffer from the desire for vengeance and a lack of forgiveness. Consider these powerful examples.

Stanley "Tookie" Williams was one of the founders of the notorious gang known as the Crips. In 1979 he was arrested for the murder of four people and served twenty-three years on death row in San Quentin prison. His life was transformed during six years of solitary confinement. He wrote several best-selling children's books, repudiating the gang lifestyle and advocating that children should choose peaceful means of settling disagreements. In 2000, he was nominated for a Nobel Peace Prize. Though killed by the state by lethal injection in 2005, Tookie "made up" with society, giving up his desire for vengeance with these words:

> I apologize to you all, children of America and South Africa, who must cope every day with dangerous street gangs. I no longer participate in the so-called gangster lifestyle, and I deeply regret that I ever did. . . . I pray that one day my apology will be accepted. I also pray that your suffering caused by gang violence will soon come to an end, as more gang members wake up and stop hurting themselves and others.[3]

Elwin Wilson had been a member of the Ku Klux Klan during the heyday of the Civil Rights movement. In 1959, he attacked and beat up John Lewis at a bus stop in Rock Hill, South Carolina, during the Civil Rights struggle. In a CNN interview on February 8, 2009, Elwin Wilson recounted his visit to Washington, DC,

Another Gang Story
Unfortunately, we often sow the wind and reap the whirlwind. Gang culture continues to abound, as demonstrated by funeral practices. At some gang-related funerals, gang members take seats set aside for biological family. They contend that they are the fallen gang member's family, and displaced biological family must sit elsewhere. Without consultation, gang leaders usurp the authority of the pastors and assume the responsibility of the pallbearers, closing out services with their own rituals and utilizing their own members and vehicles to transport the body.

in which he apologized to John Lewis, at that point a U.S. congressman from Georgia since 1987. Congressman Lewis declared that it was the power of grace and love that made Wilson's apology possible.

Yes, makin' up is a powerful thing. There's joy in the world when forgiveness is offered and accepted. That's the Jesus way, the true Advent sprit that ushers in the joy of the Christmas season.

NOTES

1. Martin Luther King, Jr., *Strength to Love* (Minneapolis: Fortress, 1982), 70.

2. James Weldon Johnson, *God's Trombones: Seven Negro Sermons in Verse* (New York: Penguin, 1990), 22-23.

3. David Muhammad, "Stanley 'Tookie' Williams Gang Leader Becomes Peace Broker." *Los Angeles Sentinel,* A-4, April 29, 2004.

Discipline Four: Makin' Time

Purpose

To help students come to understand that the most precious gift is time.

Prayer

Dear Lord God, thank you for daily makin' time for us. Teach us to be willing to make precious time for both the lovable and unlovable in our community. May we follow the example of Jesus, who was always freely giving his time and who made eternity available to all who believe. We thank you for this precious gift. In the name of this same Jesus, we pray. Amen.

Time for Others

When the angels had left them and gone into heaven, the shepherds said to one another, "Let's go to Bethlehem and see this thing that has happened, which the Lord has told us about." So they hurried off and found Mary and Joseph, and the baby, who was lying in the manger. When they had seen him, they spread the word concerning what had been told them about this child, and all who heard it were amazed at what the shepherds said to them. But Mary treasured up all these things and pondered them in her heart. (Luke 2:15-19, NIV)

After they had heard the king, they went on their way, and the star they had seen in the east went ahead of them until it stopped over the place where the child was. When they saw the star, they were overjoyed. On coming to the house, they saw the child with his mother Mary, and they bowed down and worshiped him. Then they opened their treasures and presented him with gifts of gold and of incense and of myrrh. (Matthew 2:9-11, NIV)

*A*dvent and Christmas are seasons of "makin' time" for others. After being informed by the angels, the shepherds took time from watching their flocks to go spend time with Jesus. They spent time telling others about what they had seen. The wise men spent time, first, looking for Jesus and inquiring after him. When they got to the place where Jesus was, they took the time, second, to worship him. They opened their treasures and gave him gifts. Although these two events are recounted in different Gospels and had to have happened at different times, Mary took the time to ponder, to meditate, and to think about what it all meant. Christmas is a season for makin' time to be in relationship with others. We should also make time to celebrate the meaning of Christmas.

The people in "my village" were always makin' time for me and for one another. This was especially true at Christmastime. It was so amazing. People who ordinarily wouldn't give you the time of day would treat you very differently during the Christmas season. My maternal grandfather, who was usually a stern, tough, matter-of-fact, no-nonsense, "in your face" kind of person most of the time, became quite civil and even gentle at Christmas. He would get his vintage pipe, sit, and invite me and other grandchildren to talk about things: the meaning of Christmas, what he did as a child, his family from Mooresville and Satin, Texas, and other family stories. It was a special time to find Grandpa in this mood.

My grandmother was always welcoming strangers. She entertained them as though they were members of the family. With so much family present at Christmas, it was hard to know every cousin by sight. We were sometimes dumbfounded to learn that the person with whom Grandma had been visiting so long was not an unfamiliar cousin but a complete stranger. This discipline seemed to rub off. Christmas became a time when we all found ourselves spending time with others just "shooting the breeze," talking about nothing in particular, just "makin' time."

The Gift of Time

Just as the wise men, the shepherds, and his parents had given him time and attention during that first Christmas season, Jesus modeled the discipline of "makin' time" during his life.

People were bringing little children to Jesus to have him touch them, but the disciples rebuked them. When Jesus saw this, he was indignant. He said to them, "Let the little children come to me, and do not hinder them, for the kingdom of God belongs to such as these. I tell you the truth, anyone who will not receive the kingdom of God like a little child will never enter it." And he took the children in his arms, put his hands on them and blessed them. (Mark 10:13-16, NIV)

The best gifts I received as a child growing up were neither monetary nor material. They were gifts of someone's time, time given to me for me.

- There was Mrs. Anderson, my first-grade teacher. She spent extra time helping me to finish my work. Her generous gift of time caused me to have more confidence.
- There were the ladies, mostly schoolteachers, who would volunteer their time during the summer, planning and operating vacation Bible school. This enabled children, in a community where parents had no money for vacation trips and camps, to have fun activities during the summer months.
- And there was Mrs. Tipton, our Little League baseball coach. We were the only Little League team with a female coach in the 1950's. Mrs. Tipton didn't know much about baseball, but she knew a lot about loving kids.
- My mother would take off from work to make time for school programs.
- Her mother took time to help us solve life's big problems.
- When God placed a calling to ministry in my life, it was my neighbor and first mentor, the Reverend G. W. Walker, Sr.,

who would invite me to sit with him on his front porch. We would talk and talk about God and life, pondering and treasuring, as Mary did that first Christmas, the mysteries of God.

There are many people who helped shape me and mold me by giving me the most precious gift of all, the gift of their time. Jesus, against the objections of his disciples, sat down and invited the children to come to him. Jesus took time to be with the children. He gave them what children need so desperately, the gift of the time of an appropriately interested adult.

Hank is in his eighties. On a regular basis, he reads to the children who have gotten in trouble during the day while at school. The principal of the school had noticed Hank's melodious voice while they both attended Bible study class and recruited him. The children look forward to "Mr. Hank" coming to read to them. They, as would most people, feel special because Hank has made time for them. However, the characteristics that make children so special, honesty, transparency, trust, and acceptance of others, are also what make them so vulnerable. They are snatched by pedophiles, abused and neglected by parents, left behind by school systems, victimized by poverty, and even made homeless—just like Jesus.

Jesus was always giving people his time. He gave time to the bewildered and fearful Nicodemus, who could not give Jesus the time of day; he came at night (John 3:2). Jesus crossed cultural, religious, and political lines and took the time to have conversation with the woman at the well (John 4:1-26) in broad daylight. When no one else would come near them, Jesus took the time to touch and heal lepers (Matthew 8:1-4). Jesus always made time to visit people in their homes, such as Pharisees (Luke 7:36) and friends like Mary and Martha (Luke 10:38-41). Even for a *persona non grata* such as Zacchaeus the loan shark, Jesus made time to visit him in his own home (Luke 19:1-9).

Why did Jesus spend time with people whom so many others tried to avoid for one reason or another? From a human perspective, Jesus was perhaps modeling behavior he had experienced as a young child. No doubt his mother, Mary, had told him of an Egyptian village that had taken them in when they had trouble in their lives. She told him how the villagers had welcomed them as strangers, befriended them, nurtured them, and fed them until they could find their way back home. From a divine perspective, Jesus was demonstrating that all belong to God. There is no social class, gender, or age in society that is not part of the family of God. We are all God's children. God makes time for us. We should make time for one another.

Contemporary Times

His mercy extends to those who fear him,
    from generation to generation.
He has performed mighty deeds with his arm;
    he has scattered those who are proud in their inmost thoughts.
He has brought down rulers from their thrones
    but has lifted up the humble.
He has filled the hungry with good things
    but has sent the rich away empty.
He has helped his servant Israel,
    remembering to be merciful. (Luke 1:50-54, NIV)

While the personal family practice of "makin' time" is important, church families should also practice the discipline of "makin' time" during the Christmas season. When Mary celebrated her pregnancy, she sang of how her coming child would allow people to see the mercy of God from generation to generation. The humble would be lifted and the hungry would be fed. God performs these mighty acts through the people of God. As a minister and pastor, I have seen and participated in many unique and wonderful Christmas ministries in which people have made time to be present for those in need of hospitality.

At Eastwood United Methodist Church in Fort Worth, Texas, young people in their twenties practiced hospitality by opening their homes and inviting neighborhood guests to their Christmas parties, assuring all who desired it a sense of fellowship during the holidays. At St. Paul United Methodist Church in downtown Dallas, church members initiated a ministry called "Body and Soul." With this ministry, the unique gifts of homeless persons were given a vehicle of expression through an arts program. Their gifts were showcased in the holiday activities of the arts district in the downtown community. Serving the homeless also gave all involved a greater appreciation for the Holy Family, who became homeless in the flight to Egypt.

As a leader (district superintendent in Texas) in the church, my family and I witnessed and participated in wonderful traditions of holiday bazaars and harvest festivals. In these events, all God's children brought crafts and baked goods to sell in a marketplace atmosphere. The money was used to finance helping ministries at the various churches.

Coming to Holman United Methodist Church in Los Angeles, California, we, as the pastoral family, have come to know and appreciate a vibrant Christmas Eve worship experience that makes time to hear a presentation of Handel's *Messiah*, which includes the church choir and members of the community. The church also practices hospitality through "Gifts Sunday," in which toys, clothes, and other items appropriate for children (birth to 12 years) are received during worship services. They are then distributed to nonprofit organizations serving underprivileged children in the area.

Holman's "Christmas in November" program, cosponsored by The Children And Family Collaborative, is a large celebration as well. Church members take the time to serve over 1,000 foster children and their parents a meal and give them Christmas gifts. Additionally, there are all kinds of "angel tree" programs. The one at Holman focuses on providing Christmas gifts to children whose incarcerated parents have made the request. The children are delighted to receive these gifts from their parents. The spirit of hospitality reigns as Holman partners with Central City Church of the Nazarene. We help them raise money for ministry on Los Angeles's skid row, where many homeless and poor live. They help us raise our Christmas consciousness.

Remember, You Are Refugees

The alien living with you must be treated as one of your native-born. Love him as yourself, for you were aliens in Egypt. I am the LORD your God. (Leviticus 19:34, NIV)

From ministry to the homeless, to welcoming the individual stranger, to reunion with long-lost family members, Advent and Christmas is the season to make time for others and to do what the village did for Jesus and the Holy Family in Egypt. Through their gift of hospitality, the

Figures on Refugees

UNHCR (United Nations High Commissioner for Refugees) is the refugee agency of the United Nations. According to its 2009 reports, there are 42 million displaced persons worldwide. Internally displaced persons are those who have been uprooted but remain within their own country. Refugees are persons who have fled for safety beyond national borders. Iraqis (13,200), Afghans (12,000), and Somalis (11,000) top the list of those seeking asylum in industrialized countries. Violence and political instability are the principal reasons for displacement. Many Americans feel displaced from the job market by people coming in. African Americans should remember that their ancestors were once the ultimate displaced persons, separated from home, loved ones, language, and culture, due to violence and political instability.

villagers of Egypt gave God's plan a helping hand. A child and family were given refuge from a dream-killer named Herod.

Our world today is saturated with a refugee problem. Refugees go from all over the world to other parts of the world. Many flee to America. They flee for the same reasons as the Holy Family: fear for their lives, lack of safety, need for protection. Advent is a time for practicing the gift of hospitality modeled by those Egyptian villagers. What a gift they gave to the world in offering refuge to the Holy Family! Many go, like Mary and Joseph, with their children. What are we to do? Indeed, the writer of Ecclesiastes, in chapter three, reminds us that there is a time and season for everything. Do like the villagers in Egypt and offer refuge and assistance. Do like Jesus and make time for the refugees among us:

> Time to sit and listen and hear their stories,
> Time to reach out and touch their pain,
> Time to talk with them to show we care,
> Time to sing their songs,
> Time to dance their dances,
> Time to laugh and time to cry with them.

There are still dream-killers among us. There are gang leaders, dope dealers, criminals, greedy CEO's, comfort-zoned Christmases, do-nothing churches, prosperity-preaching Pharisees, lazy saints—all dream-killers. Overtly or covertly, unintentionally or intentionally, innocuously or blatantly, whether with knives, bullets, dope, lifestyles that diminish well-being, insensitivity, neglect, or greed, dreams get killed. We are all refugees looking for the fully realized kingdom of God. As Christians, we await the second coming of Christ to experience the reign of God in its fullness.

Jesus was hard on dream-killers (Matthew 23; 25). He spent his time fighting for, saving, and protecting people from dream-killers who would use the religious, social, and/or government systems to oppress those who could not fight for themselves. The Egyptian villagers did it for him, and he used his time to do it for others. Jesus wanted everyone to experience the fullness of God's grace, which would allow for the possibility of reaching

Who Is a Dream-killer?

Those in leadership roles have great power for good or evil. They can build up a dream or tear it down. Jesus includes many scribes and Pharisees as dream-killers, persons who create barriers to well-being for others. "They tie up heavy burdens, hard to bear, and lay them on the shoulders of others; but they themselves are unwilling to lift a finger to move them" (Matthew 23:4, NRSV). Jesus goes on to accuse these religious leaders of locking people out of the kingdom of heaven (verse 13), of making minor issues into major stumbling blocks (verses 16-24), and of focusing on the outside appearance rather than the internal spirit (verses 25-28).

Jesus was equal in his condemnation of dream-killers, no matter who was at fault. In Matthew 25, he tells stories about those who kill their own dreams. Five of ten bridesmaids do not bring enough oil to meet the bridegroom. They are unable to accomplish their dream of going into the wedding feast due to lack of preparation (verses 1-13). One man buries the foundational material given him by his boss, in effect killing the possibility for growth, killing his own dream (verses 14-30). Finally, in verses 31-46, Jesus makes it clear that dream-killers are those who do nothing to promote the flourishing of others. Those who do not feed the hungry, clothe the naked, visit the prisoners, and so on are all dream-killers.

one's God-given potential. The rich African soil of *ubuntu*, from which the Savior of the world emerged, embodies this ethic. The spirit of *ubuntu* is grounded in "a socio–economic system that placed the emphasis on sharing and giving, rather than on self-aggrandisement and getting."[1]

Yes, Advent is a season of "makin' time" for others. There is an old rhyme of yesteryear:

> We have only just one minute,
> Only sixty seconds in it,
> Forced upon me—can't refuse it,
> Didn't seek it, didn't choose it,
> But it's up to me to use it,
> I must suffer if I lose it,
> Give account if I abuse it,
> Just a tiny little minute,
> But eternity is in it.

Don't settle for a Christmas where money and materialism is your rule. That's not the spirit of Christmas hospitality and that certainly is not *ubuntu*! Besides, money is so woefully inadequate.

Money can buy some books but not an education.
Money can buy a bed but not sleep.
Money can buy a Bible but not religion.
Money can buy a computer but not common sense.
Money can buy clothes but not character.
Money can buy lingerie but not love.
Money can buy a following but not friends.
Money can buy sex but not a soul mate.
Money can buy security but not a savior.
Money can buy treasure but not time.

You only have sixty seconds. What are you waiting for? This Christmas season, go find someone with whom to share your most precious gift: time!

NOTE

1. Desmond Tutu, *Crying in the Wilderness*, 100.

*T*he villagers in Egypt celebrated our Lord's birth by offering hospitality to his family. They accommodated the Holy Family at a time when they needed help, safety, love, and acceptance. They practiced *ubuntu*. Jesus responded with a life that did the same. He took the gift of hospitality, mingled it with his holy blood, and brought joy to the world. The African village and Jesus took the steps that made the world better. They demonstrated what happens when love for God pushes us out of our comfort zones, so that, even as we may look different and act differently depending on racial and cultural backgrounds, we can begin to allow for differences and, respecting them, love one another until our perceived differences no longer make a difference.

Perhaps this Christmas season is your time to begin or extend your tradition of hospitality. The Egyptian village that welcomed Jesus was part of the plan of deliverance that started with the crossing of the Red Sea by the Hebrew children, continued through the deliverance of black people from slavery in America and the collapse of apartheid in South Africa, and continues to this day in the way God intervenes in and interacts with history to promote human flourishing. As followers of Jesus, we must constantly put forth every effort to find ways to break through walls that prevent deliverance in our families, our communities, and our churches. Our world needs it and our faith demands it.

Advent/Christmas has often become a time when so many "things" overshadow the sacred meaning of the birth of our Lord. Innocently and innocuously, we participate in and even encourage many sacrilegious and outrageous practices.

> We eat too much.
> We shop too much.
> We spend too much.
> We drink too much.
> We party too much.
> We fight too much.

This Advent/Christmas season, make your place a space where you make room for others, emotionally and physically; make do with what you have, whether in times of abundance or scarcity; make up with those who need to hear a reconciling word from you; and make time for those who need it most. May others receive from you what Jesus and the Holy Family received from the Egyptian village: the gift of hospitality!

MAKIN' ROOM IN THE INN: CHRISTMAS HOSPITALITY THROUGH AN AFRICAN AMERICAN EXPERIENCE

Preparing to Teach

*T*he leader guide is included to help those who are facilitating this study for adult learners. Each session includes a purpose, meditation, and prayer to help the leader spiritually prepare. The purpose and prayer are included at the front of each student lesson as well. However, the meditation can be shared to open up each class time if so desired by the leader. It might be the simplest thing for the leader just to read the meditation and have the group reflect silently for a few seconds. Then allow a participant to read the purpose and another to read the prayer.

Discussion questions are found in the leader guide alone. The leader may formulate his/her own questions. Additionally, questions may arise from within the group. Invite participants to meditate on these questions. Encourage students to use their biblical knowledge and insights. Ask them to be concise in describing their experiences and telling their stories so that several people can contribute. You may want to allow them to share as partners or in small groups, and sometimes there are directions to do so. However, conduct the sessions in the way most comfortable for your community. The leader may have the students turn to the appropriate to be able to read them for clarity. The leader may, however, choose to write the questions on a blackboard, a whiteboard, or on a flipchart so that all may see together without having to flip pages.

The leader guide includes a section not found in the student pages, "Living Out Ubuntu." The leader should allot enough time for these more in-depth summarizing discussion questions, in that they will help participants begin to formulate an action plan that brings to life the lessons learned for each hospitality discipline.

For effective facilitation, the leader should read every part of the lesson in advance of the group's meeting. While this is an all-inclusive resource, during group time, the only person who must flip from the lesson pages to the leader pages will be the leader. Knowledge of what the pages contain will enable the leader to move between the guide and the lesson with ease.

The material in the boxes of the student lessons contains additional information that may help to clarify particular sections of the lesson. Have them read these sections aloud, depending on the interest of the class and on the time. You may want to summarize some of what is in the boxes and simply tell students to read them word for word in the course of their review and/or preparation.

Session One

Leader Preparation

1. Prepare by reading the Introduction and the entire lesson titled "Makin' Room," including the meditation, all boxes, and Scripture references.
2. Review the study and discussion questions and decide which ones to include during the time you have.
3. Be mindful that because Session One includes the reading of the Introduction, the time for discussion may be more limited.

Meditation

Through the birth of Jesus Christ, God demonstrated ultimate hospitality toward humankind. Jesus was the means through which God was reconciling the entire world to himself. Our Savior, that sweet little Jesus boy, was treated so mean. He knows about being the stranger. He knows about being the refugee. He knows about seeking safety and flourishing somewhere else besides home. And he still loved everybody, even those who treated him so meanly. Desmond Tutu, Martin Luther King, Jr., and Howard Thurman all taught that Christians have no choice but to love because it is how Jesus lived, what Jesus taught, and what he requires. We can trust Jesus because he knows all about the struggle of being a loving human being in an unloving world. However, through the strength of his love, we too have the power to love the totality of humankind.

The Introduction

Opening *(10 minutes)*

1. Allow each person to introduce himself or herself and share a reason for why they are in the study.
2. Have the words to the spiritual "Sweet Little Jesus Boy" read aloud (p. 7).
3. Ask someone to read the Introduction (p. 7).
4. Help students have a working understanding of *ubuntu* theology. Please note that while the reference given utilizes the "ub<u>a</u>ntu" spelling, the most recent writings use "ub<u>u</u>ntu."

Discipline One: Makin' Room (p. 11)

Opening *(5 minutes)*
1. Have someone read the purpose of the lesson.
2. You may choose to include a reading of the meditation.
3. Invite the group to pray. You may choose to utilize the prayer in the lesson.

Purpose

To help students think about cultivating and living out hospitality between the diversity of God's people

Prayer

Dear Lord, may the love you shower upon us during this season enlarge our spirits and our hearts, that we may in turn share the gift of Christian love with others. In Jesus' name. Amen.

An American Village *(10 minutes)*; p. 11
1. Have someone read the Bible passage (Luke 2:4-7).
2. Have the group read this section.
3. Highlight any information from the boxes you feel will help the group have more insight. You can do this by sharing yourself or by having a participant read from the box you choose.
4. Invite participants to meditate on these questions. Encourage students to use their biblical knowledge and insights. Ask them to be concise in describing their experiences and telling their stories so that several people can contribute. You may want to allow them to share as partners or in small groups.
   a. What do you think it was like for Joseph, Mary, and the baby Jesus to be turned away by the motel manager that night?
   b. What are your experiences of being turned away?

The African Village *(15 minutes)*; p. 14
1. Have someone read the Bible passage (Matthew 2:14-15).
2. Have the participants take turns reading this section aloud.
3. Point out to group members any information in the boxes that may be helpful.

4. Invite participants to answer these questions.
  a. What are unique lessons/experiences Africans and African Americans offer to the world?
  b. What is the difference between the "rugged individualism" so popular in American culture and an ubuntu perspective?

The Village of God's Kingdom *(15 minutes)*; p. 18

1. Have someone read the Bible passage (John 14:2).
2. Get two people to read the first paragraph. Have them alternate reading each sentence in the list. Depending on your time constraints, choose to have two or three of the shorter passages in the list read by a third person.
3. Allow the group to share in finishing the section.
4. Divide the larger group into three smaller groups and assign one of the questions below to each group for discussion.
  a. Who are the people in your circle of family and friends that are on the fringes of the community?
  b. What models do we have for living in such a diverse world?
  c. How are we able to see people of different races and cultures as brother and sister?

Living Out Ubuntu *(15 minutes)*

1. Write the questions in large lettering where all can see them.
2. Divide the class into three groups.
3. Assign one question to each group.
4. Challenge each group to come up with at least one plan of action in relationship to one of these questions.
  a. What are the most important lessons to be learned from this study session?
  b. What can we do to help "make room" in our families, our churches, our corporations, our world?
  c. How might Christmas in your home, church, and/or community be different this year after this discussion?
5. Offer closing remarks and thank all for coming.
6. Offer a closing prayer.
7. Remind the group to study for the upcoming lesson.

Session Two

1. Pray and then read the chapter titled "Makin Do."
2. Read the meditation.
3. Research the works of Dr. Lerone Bennett, such as *Before the Mayflower*. They include descriptors and definitions of the "genius of survival."
4. Read the Scripture lessons and commentary about the texts.
5. Review the discussion questions and think about possible answers to help facilitate the discussion period.

Meditation

Jesus was born into poverty. His first bed was a manger. His teenage mother was not able to afford the required Temple offering. Extreme poverty continues to exist all over the world. However, we can see the "genius of survival" in the offering African villagers collected for the survivors of Katrina in New Orleans. Their graciousness demonstrated ubuntu hospitality toward their fellow human beings, who, though living in a land of plenty, were experiencing extreme lack. The Advent and Christmas seasons provide many opportunities to exercise and demonstrate gracious hospitality to those in need. As we collect our hand-me-downs to share with those struggling to survive, let us remember that the humanity of our Lord is reflected in the humanity of those who still live a hand-me-down existence. Let us never forget that in comparison to God, we are all poor in what is most needed, and be thankful for God's all-sufficient grace.

Discipline Two: Makin' Do (p. 21)

Opening *(5 minutes)*
1. Have someone read the purpose of the lesson.
2. You may choose to include a reading of the meditation, but be sure to open in prayer.

Purpose

To help students experience Advent from the perspective of "makin' do," which is about trusting God as compared to trusting in wealth.

Prayer

Dear Lord God, we thank you for always being sufficient for our every need. Help us to be like Paul, knowing that although we may be in need, we can live as though we have plenty. We ask this in the precious name of Jesus, our Christ. Amen.

Jesus Was Poor *(10 minutes)*; p. 21

1. Have two participants alternate in reading the Scripture (Luke 2:21-24 and Leviticus 12:6, 8) and the lesson text of this section.
2. Divide the group into three smaller groups and assign one question to each for discussion.
   a. Did you realize that Mary might have been as young as 14 years when she became pregnant? Does this alter your view of Mary or about the Christ event?
   b. Would Jesus' socioeconomic status as a poor Jew enable him to relate better with the poor and marginalized people of his day? of our day?
   c. What has been your experience of poverty? Did you grow up poor? Do you have relationships with anyone who was/is poor?

A Hand-Me-Down Society *(15 minutes)*; p. 23

1. Have someone read the Bible passage (Luke 4:18-19).
2. Have the group take turns reading this section aloud.
3. Point out to group members any information in the boxes that may be helpful.
4. Ask the group: What else would you add to the "hand-me-down" list in this lesson? What's the effect on people who have had to accept secondhand things?

The Genius of Survival *(15 minutes)*; p. 26

1. Have someone read the biblical passages (Matthew 2:13; Exodus 1:12).

2. Have participants take turns reading the section, including the box material.
3. Make this statement: African Americans were referred to as having "the genius of survival." Having read about this characteristic, what does it mean to you? How does this relate to the story of Mary and Joseph?

Our Situation Versus God's Destination *(10 minutes)*; p. 28

1. Read Philippians 4:11 for the class. Ask: How is this Scripture "lived out" in your life today?
2. Continue with the rest of the section.

Angels and Friends *(5 minutes)*; p. 30

After reading this section, go to "Living Out Ubuntu."

Living Out Ubuntu *(5 minutes)*

1. Ask: What is the most important thing we can do for/with the poor and those forced to "make do" with so little in our churches, communities, cities, world? What is the difference in doing something *for* others as opposed to doing something *with* them?
2. On a board or flipchart, make a list of the ministries in which your church participates that help the poor in your community survive and thrive.
3. Offer closing remarks and thank all for coming.
4. Offer a closing prayer.
5. Remind the group to study for the upcoming lesson.

Session Three

Leader Preparation

1. Pray and then read the chapter titled "Makin' Up."
2. Read the meditation.
3. Take a few moments to remember your favorite family reunion. Be prepared to share these memories with participants.
4. You may want to do some research on St. Augustine.
5. Read the Scriptures and be prepared to define the difference between forgiveness and reconnection or reconciliation.

Meditation

Jesus' teaching on forgiveness may seem impossible; however, it reminds us of God's great gift to us. It is because of God's forgiveness that we are able to receive the gifts of the Advent season. Those who follow the discipline of Jesus Christ are required to forgive. It is a great blessing because it enables families and communities to move towards wholeness and to a welcoming spirit for those who may be hard to love. It has been noted that African peoples are the most forgiving people on earth. Perhaps the heritage of ubuntu is helpful in the practice of this discipline of "makin' up." In this season, let us grow in our ability to be inclusive, rather than exclusive, in our families and our communities.

Discipline Three: Makin' Up (p. 31)

Opening *(10 minutes)*
1. Have someone read the purpose of the lesson.
2. Have the group read the prayer in unison.
3. Allow participants to share memories about family reunions. There have been many films that deal with the subject of families getting together (*The Family Stone, Madea's Family Reunion, Johnson Family Reunion, Four Christmases, Welcome Home, Roscoe Jenkins*). The class may choose to discuss elements of these in talking about families getting together.

Purpose

To help students come to understand the importance of forgiveness and reconnection, especially in the season of Advent.

Prayer

Dear God, thank you for your forgiveness. Help us to honor you by having an attitude of forgiveness toward family and community during this season of Advent. In the matchless name of Jesus, the baby of the manger. Amen.

Reunion *(15 minutes)*; p. 31
1. Have the class read the biblical passage (Matthew 2:19-21).
2. After they have taken turns reading the section, allow participants to discuss the following statements:
   a. Do most people who leave home have an innate desire, a spiritual longing, to go back home?
   b. What are your personal experiences of "going back" home or having someone return back home?

Forgiveness *(15 Minutes)*; p. 33
1. Have someone read the biblical passage (Matthew 5:43-48).
2. After the section has been read, ask each person to choose a partner (the person sitting beside them) in order to discuss the questions.
   a. How do the biblical passages in this section show that forgiveness was foundational to Jesus' teachings?
   b. Christmas is a very special time in Christian communities/families. We are implored to have the "Christmas spirit." How does the "embrace of the forgiveness ethos" impact your family tradition in demonstrating "the Christmas spirit"?

Back Home *(15 minutes)*; p. 35
1. Ask a participant to read the first two paragraphs of this section.
2. Ask: Which of the African proverbs listed in this section resonate with your understanding of Christian principles?
3. Have someone continue reading the section.

Makin' Up Is Hard to Do *(20 minutes)*; p. 36

1. Read the box about James Weldon Johnson.
2. Choose two people to read this section. One will read the Scripture passages; the other will read the text.
3. At the end of the section, ask: Beyond forgiveness, what other qualities are included in "makin' up"?

The Power of Makin' Up *(10 minutes)*; p. 39

1. After the story about Stanley "Tookie" Williams is read, read the box titled "Another Gang Story." Invite participants to share experiences with gang culture.
2. After the story is read about Elvin Wilson, invite participants to share experiences with racism.

Living Out Ubuntu *(5 minutes)*

1. What role can Christians have in bringing forgiveness to situations of violence and racism?
2. What opportunities and/or challenges do you foresee this Christmas in your family?
3. Offer closing remarks and thank all for coming.
4. Offer a closing prayer.
5. Remind the group to study for the upcoming lesson.

Session Four

Leader Preparation

1. Pray and then read the chapter titled "Makin' Time."
2. Read and personally reflect upon the discussion questions in the guide.
3. Read the Scriptures and relate them to contemporary life.

Meditation

The baby Jesus was a refugee. He and his parents were displaced persons. Perhaps this is one reason why he was so empathetic with persons who seemed out of place. Who are the refugees among us, those who are always out of place? Children are often treated as displaced persons, to seen and not heard in an adult world. From the time he began his ministry, Jesus became displaced, not accepted in his hometown. Out of place, displaced with no place to lay his head. During Advent, as we celebrate the birth of the ultimate displaced person, the one who left his home in glory to walk the earth, taking time to sit and listen to our stories, to reach out and touch our pain, to speak without judgment, it is a good time for us to take the time to be with the displaced: the children, the refugee, the foster child, those in nursing homes. By showing that we care, exchanging songs, sorrows, and stories, we imitate the actions of the shepherds and wise men who made the time to worship one newly displaced in a stable. Sharing the gift of time goes a long way in giving people a sense of home and belonging. What a great gift for the Advent season!

Discipline Four: Makin' Time (p. 41)

Opening *(5 minutes)*
1. Have someone read the purpose of the lesson.
2. Have a participant offer a prayer either by reading the one in the lesson or creating his/her own.

Purpose

To help students come to understand that the most precious gift is time.

Prayer

Dear Lord God, thank you for daily makin' time for us. Teach us to be willing to make precious time for both the lovable and unlovable in our community. May we follow the example of Jesus, who was always freely giving his time and who made eternity available to all who believe. We thank you for this precious gift. In the name of this same Jesus, we pray. Amen.

Time for Others *(20 minutes)*; p. 41
1. Select two persons to read the Scripture passages (Luke 2:15-19 and Matthew 2:9-11).
2. Choose another person to read the lesson text.
3. Invite the class into a period of discussion by making this statement: Mary and the wise men remind us how valuable it is to take time "to ponder" and to share gifts and worship in community.
4. Ask these questions.
   a. What are the memorable experiences in your family tradition of Christmas that reflect the value of spending time together in worship, exchanging gifts, meals, service to others, and so on?
   b. Name some of the people with whom you spent this special time with at Christmas season.

The Gift of Time *(10 minutes)*; p. 43
1. Have someone read the first two paragraphs, including the section that contains the Scripture.
2. Invite participants to share a memory concerning someone who spent time with them as children.
3. After reading the third paragraph, invite the class to talk about current events concerning the lives of children.
   a. How are children victimized, made hopeless, or otherwise discarded in today's world?
   b. Jesus spent time with children. What is a favorite childhood experience of someone being Jesus to you at Christmas?

Contemporary Times *(15 minutes)*; p. 45

1. Ask a participant to read the Scripture (Luke 1:50-54).
2. Ask the group to read the rest of the section silently.
3. Allow them to share their memories. Make sure that you take the opportunity to allow sharing in the second part of the question, remembering that all people did not have church experience as children.
   a. Churches have many unique and meaningful Christmas traditions. What are some of the Christmas traditions you celebrated in your church as a child?
   b. As an adult?

Remember, You Are Refugees *(10 minutes)*; p. 46

1. After reading the Scripture and the first two paragraphs, be sure to have participants look at the information in the box.
2. Ask: What is your attitude towards immigrants and refugees? Do you know any personally? Have you been a refugee? Are you an immigrant?
3. Have the class read the next two paragraphs dealing with "dream-killers." If there is time, have someone read the box material summarizing Matthew 23 and 25.
4. Have participants create a definition for "dream-killer." Write it for all to see.
5. Complete the lesson text and allow comment on the list of proverbs about money.

Living Out Ubuntu

1. What have you learned from this study that will help you deepen the meaning of your Christmas?
2. Have you developed a deeper sense of what it means to be hospitable?
3. What are some of the other stories you have heard from participants that will help you to enrich with your own family tradition?
4. Offer closing remarks: As we have learned through this study, our precious Savior and his family were given hospitality by an Egyptian village. Like the Holy Family, many today need hospitality

extended to them in order to survive. As those who follow Christ, we are called to practice hospitality.

5. Thank all for coming and remind them of any continuing projects they may have decided to do.

6. Offer a closing prayer.